Treasure Coins of the
Nuestra Señora de Atocha
& the *Santa Margarita*

Carol Tedesco

SeaStory Press
Key West, Florida

Treasure Coins of the Nuestra Señora de Atocha and the Santa Margarita
© Carol Tedesco 2010
All rights reserved

Library of Congress Cataloging in Publication Data
Tedesco, Carol.
    Treasure coins of the Nuestra Senora de Atocha and the Santa Margarita / Carol Tedesco.
        p. cm.
    Includes bibliographical references.
    ISBN 978-0-9821151-8-3
    1. Coins, Spanish--Catalogs. 2. Coins, Latin American--Catalogs. 3. Silver coins--Catalogs. 4. Nuestra Senora de Atocha (Ship) 5. Santa Margarita (Ship) 6. Treasure troves--Florida. 7. Shipwrecks--Florida. 8. Mints--Bolivia--Potosi--History. 9. Mints--Mexico--Mexico City--History. 10. Mints--Peru--Lima--History. I. Title.
    CJ3189.T33 2010
    737.4946--dc22
                                                            2010044676

SeaStory Press
305 Whitehead St.
Key West Florida 33040
book design by Sheri Lohr, SeaStory Press
    Notes on fonts: The body of this book is set in Cochin, based on the work of the 18th century French engraver Charles-Nicolas Cochin. The title page features Caslon Antique, created by American Berne Nadall in 1896-98 and named for 18th century English punchcutter William Caslon. The font Blackadder, featured on page headers and the title page was created in 1996 by British designer Bob Anderton, inspired by the confession signature of infamous insurrectionist, Guy Fawkes.

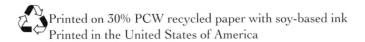Printed on 30% PCW recycled paper with soy-based ink
Printed in the United States of America

Dedicated With Love
to Daniel Tedesco
Father, Editor, Mentor

Table of Contents

Prelude 1

Treasures of the Atocha and the Santa Margarita 2

Origins 3

The Spanish Dollar 4

What Would a "Piece of Eight" Buy in the 17th Century? . . . 6

Cleaning Shipwreck-Recovered Coins 6

Grading Shipwreck-Recovered Coins 7

Coins of the Potosi Mint 9

Assayers of the Potosi Mint 14

Coins of the Mexico City Mint 16

Assayers of the Mexico City Mint 18

Coins of the Lima, Peru Mint 20

Assayers of the Lima, Peru Mint 22

Table of Contents

Exceedingly Rare Mint Specimens ~ New World 23

Exceedingly Rare Mint Specimens ~ Old World 25

Exceedingly Rare Mint Specimens ~ Gold Coins 28

Acknowledgements 29

Suggested Reading 31

Recommended Web Sites 32

Image Credits 32

About the Author 33

Prelude

Since people first began trading with one another for goods and goodies, money - in one form or another - truly has made "the world go around." Today we go online to move money – sometimes lots of it – from place to place, but not so terribly long ago money was transported on wooden ships, and though these ships are often romantically memorialized as "golden galleons," prior to the California gold-rush of the mid-eighteen hundreds, they were in truth silver galleons.

With a desperate need for money and a conviction of entitlement to acquire it at any cost, the kingdom of Spain's approach was to plunder the resources of others. By 1622, little more than 100 years after the first voyage of Christopher Columbus, Spain's boundless lust for riches - and glory, and souls to convert - had resulted in the conquest of much of the Caribbean, Mexico, and the Americas. Silver was the most abundant treasure of the "Indies" and royal mints were established to control and regulate a seemingly inexhaustible torrent of mineral wealth pouring from the mines. By 1622, New World silver in the form of the Spanish dollar was the most coveted and widely traded money on earth.

The Conquest of Tenochtitlán,
oil on canvas, artist unknown, second half of the 17th century

Treasures of the Atocha and the Santa Margarita

Photo by Don Kincaid
A portion of the lower hull section of the Atocha, as witnessed by divers Greg Wareham and Andy Matroci. Blackened circular coins are clearly visible in deteriorated rectangular wooden chests. Matroci recalls biting the mouthpiece off of his regulator at the moment of discovery.

On July 20, 1985, two divers working for treasure hunter Mel Fisher discovered a dark, irregularly shaped, and mysterious mass rising from the ocean floor in 55 feet of seawater near the Marquesas Keys in the Florida Straits. It was the lower hull section of the 1622 *Tierra Firme* fleet galleon *Nuestra Señora de Atocha*—an estimated $400 million find.

Five years prior, and three miles away, members of Fisher's team had discovered a portion of the *Atocha's* sister ship, the *Santa Margarita*. These two treasure galleons were destroyed within sight of one another in the Florida Straits on September 6, 1622, victims—as a contemporaneous account related—of a "storme and fearfull tempest." Spilling from their smashed and broken hulls were tens of thousands of silver "pieces of eight" treasure coins—the lifeblood of the Spanish empire.

Origins

Though treasures of all descriptions imaginable continue to be recovered from these widely dispersed shipwrecks, fewer than 180,000 coins have been recovered from the *Atocha* shipwreck to date, and fewer than 50,000 from the *Santa Margarita*. As coin cargo of *Tierra Firme* fleet ships, most originated from the mint of the city of Potosi; then a territory of the Viceroyalty of Peru, today of Bolivia, and most were minted during the reign of King Philip III. Other mints and time periods are represented as well, but these are considered particular rarities within the *Atocha/Margarita* collections.

Examples of 1622 *Tierra Firme* rarities include coins with full or partial dates, Mexico City mint coins, and coins minted during the reign of King Philip II. Designated as "early" coins, those minted during the reign of Philip II were already relatively old when the fleet sailed, and were produced during an era of great pride in craftsmanship and less urgency to make money fast. The men responsible for producing them were skilled artisans — jewelers, silversmiths, and engravers who crafted coins that were centered, symmetrical, and finely detailed.

More rare still are coins minted in the reign of King Philip IV, whose rule began in March of 1621; coins displaying the legend of Johanna and Charles I, who ruled from 1504-1556; and the exquisitely lovely Lima, Peru, mint coins. Exceedingly rare specimens are one reale coins from any mint, coins from the Panama mint, the Santa Fe de Bogotá and Cartagena, Colombia mints; and a small representation of Old World minted coins, including the mints of Seville, Old Granada, Toledo, Madrid, and Segovia. These are the treasures within the treasure.

The Spanish Dollar

A 16th century woodcut provides a glimpse into the workings of a mint; blanks being cut from sheets of silver, struck into coins, weighed and documented.

Every coin that came out of every mint in the Americas until the 1700s was made one at a time, by hand, so each is unique. To make coins in the 16th and 17th centuries, blanks were hand-cut from strips of silver. A heated blank, or planchet, was then sandwiched between double dies, and struck with a hammer. Any silver in excess of the requisite weight was trimmed from the outer edges of the coin until the weight was correct. This resulted in irregularly shaped coins whose insignia were often off-center. The dies themselves were made of steel, with insignia impressed into them by direct engraving or by the sinking (stamping) of multiple die punches, each punch being a component of the coin's design. Just as when two different artists paint an image using the same model, or pattern, the symbols engraved into the dies reflect the artistic individuality of each engraver.

8 Reales   4 Reales   2 Reales   1 Reale

[Coin images in this book are shown at approximately actual size.]

The Spanish Dollar

Coin denominations are counted in reales. There have been four sizes, or denominations, of silver coins discovered on the Atocha and Santa Margarita shipwrecks to date. In quantities found, eight reales coins have been by far the most abundant, followed by four reales, then two reales, with one reale coins being scarce.

- Eight reales of silver equaled the one-ounce Spanish silver dollar of approximately 27.2 grams—less than the troy ounce standard today.
- Four reales coins, at ½ ounce each, are half the weight and were half the value of the eight reales coin.
- At ¼ ounce, two reales coins are half the weight and were half the value of four reales coins.
- Lastly, at 1/8 ounce, the exceedingly rare one reale coin is half the weight and was half the value of the two reales coin, having 1/8th the value of the eight reales coin.
- There is no record of any ½ or ¼ reale coins having been recovered from any of the 1622 fleet vessels, though these denominations were produced intermittently throughout the Spanish Colonial period.

The value of money was determined by the purity and weight of the metal. That being the case, it was not uncommon at the time to cut coins into pieces and weigh the pieces to make change—hence the origin of the money's legendary nickname, *"pieces of eight."*

What Would a "Piece of Eight" Buy in the 17th Century?

The value depends largely upon whom you ask. While it is widely quoted that a common workingman would labor one month for a Spanish dollar, just like today the value of money fluctuates as a result of factors including inflation, recession, and geography. An example depictive of the times can be found in the Pirate's Articles of agreement, detailed in John Esquemeling's 17th century chronicle, *The Buccaneers of America*. Esquemeling wrote, "Lastly, they stipulate in writing what recompense or reward each one ought to have, that is either wounded or maimed in his body, suffering the loss of any limb, by that voyage. Thus they order for the loss of a right arm six hundred pieces of eight, or six slaves; for the loss of a left arm five hundred pieces of eight, or five slaves; for a right leg five hundred pieces of eight, or five slaves..."

Cleaning Shipwreck-Recovered Coins

Because of a chemical reaction between the metal and the salt water, a residue of silver called silver sulfide forms, blackening the coins, and fusing them together in the shape of the wooden chests that once held them. Blackened and encrusted silver shipwreck recovered coins are cleaned by a technique called electrolytic reduction—along with lots of elbow grease. First, coins are separated from the conglomeration, and then suspended individually from metal alligator clips into a tub of soda ash and water. The alligator clips are secured to rods with stainless steel wire, and the rods are wired to a battery, with voltage and amperage determined by the number of coins in each batch. Next, the power supply is engaged, beginning a process of reverse electrolysis. After cleaning, each coin is studied, photographed, documented, graded, and certified.

Grading Shipwreck-Recovered Coins

Coins are graded by quality, and in the case of shipwreck-recovered coins, quality is largely determined by degree of exposure to the elements.

Grade One coins, those having little or no visible ocean wear, mostly come from the interior of treasure chests or conglomerations. They show little or no roughness or pitting, looking much as they did when new. Both sides are in Very Good to Excellent condition, and the obverse and reverse features resulting from the original strike are defined and easily identifiable.

Grade Two coins were partly exposed to the elements. The coin may not be completely intact, or it may look more "sandblasted" than a Grade One, but the quality is still Good, and most of the features resulting from the original strike are easily identifiable.

Grade Three coins are in Fair over-all condition, but ocean wear is very apparent. Many Grade Three coins were on the outer layer of a treasure chest and therefore the side of the coin that faced into the chest will be of Grade One or Grade Two quality, while the opposite side, the one that faced the elements, is completely worn away. Other Grade Three coins might have ocean wear distributed across both sides of the coin. On Grade Three coins, obverse and/or reverse sides will still offer easily identifiable characteristics that have definition.

Grade Four coins are still identifiable as a Spanish Colonial coin, but they have been subject to much wear and tear, and the markings are faint and have little or no definition.

Grade Five coins are just above a fragment in quality. You can identify it as a coin, taking into consideration factors such as shape and provenance.

There will be areas of "soft strike"— smooth areas that appear as though the markings have been erased—on almost all handmade coins. Often, this is due to the blanks of silver used to make the coins not being uniformly flat, as well as coin dies that wore down unevenly with use over time. It can also be the result of tongs that were used to hold the coins during production. Soft strike should not be confused with ocean wear, which can make a coin look rough, pitted, or sand-blasted. Since a soft strike still represents the "mint" condition of a coin, provided such areas are not excessive, it does not diminish the value of a coin.

Example of Soft Strike

Coins of the Potosi Mint

Since the vast majority of the coins discovered on the *Atocha* and the *Santa Margarita* were minted in Potosi, it makes sense to learn about Potosi mint coins first. Once the reader is familiar with the features of these coins, it is not difficult to apply this knowledge, with some modifications, to those produced in other mints.

Potosi Mint Coin Obverse and Reverse

The crowned shield side of a Potosi mint coin is the front, and is called the obverse. The reverse displays the lions of Léon and the castles of Castile, quartered by the Greek cross and surrounded by a curving Moorish design called a tressure, or quatrefoil. On either side, the symbols are encircled within dots and a legend:

PHILIPVS III D.G. HISPANIARVM ET INDIARVM REX ANO

This means, Philip III By the Grace of God (Dei Gratia) Spain and the Indies King, In the Year of Our Lord (Ano Domeni) 16—.

The letter "U" is presented as "V" in the classical Latin style.

Potosi coins minted during the reign of Philip II did not carry a date and do not display an ordinal number, so the legend will read:

PHILIPVS D.G. HISPANIARVM ET INDIARVM REX.

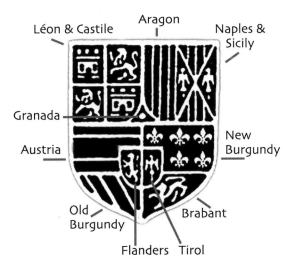

The shield pictured is the Hapsburg Shield, the arms of King Philip III of Spain, and, with some variations, of the other Hapsburg Kings: Philip II, Philip IV, and Charles II. The symbols that compose the shield are the various individual arms of lands under Spanish rule at the time. So, the shield side of the coin represents the power of Spain, and when the power changed, the shield changed as well.

Coin Shield Quadrants

1. The lions and castles in the upper-left quadrant represent Léon and Castile, respectively.

2. The vertical lines in the top-center represent Aragon.

3. The upper-right quadrant represents Naples and Sicily.

4. The solid raised horizontal bar in the left-center represents Austria.

5. The fleurs-de-lis represent New Burgundy.

6. The lion in the lower right represents Brabant, now part of Germany.

7. The diagonal lines in the lower left represent Old Burgundy.

8. The small pomegranate represents New Granada.

9. The lion and the falcon side-by-side represent Flanders and Tirol, respectively.

To the left of the shield, typically, are two initials, one over the other—though placement of elements can vary. The upper initial on a Potosi mint coin will be a "P" for Potosi, or Peru. Below the letter "P" the chief assayer of the mint was required to place his own initial, therefore, this letter changes. Because assayers came and went over time, and sometimes substituted for one another, it is not uncommon to detect initial over-strikes and "erasures."

To the right of the shield is a numeral expressing the coin's value. This value can appear in the form of traditional Roman numerals or in a manner that reflected the handwritten style of the times, which often included an "o" above the value; or in the Arabic form.

Coins that display a date are rare because, though the Potosi mint opened in 1573, dates were not introduced into the legend until the year 1617. When the date was eventually added to Potosi mint coin dies, it was located at about the 11 o'clock position on the outer perimeter of the reverse. Because the coins were hand struck and hand cut, most of the wording in the legends and most of the dates were cut off in the process of obtaining the desired weight.

Potosí mint, small monogrammed assayer initials RL/RBL, 4 reales coin circa 1589-1598

Potosí mint, curved monogrammed assayer initials RB/RL/RBL, 2 reales coin circa 1598-1610, with visible ordinal III

Potosí mint, assayer Q, 8 reales coin circa 1613-1616, stars replace fleur-de-lys

Coins of the Potosi Mint

Key West artist Kate Peachey's interpretation of a detail from the first printed sketch of Potosi, from Pedro de Cieza de León's *La cronica del Peru*, Seville, 1553.

Treasure Coins ◊ Carol Tedesco

Assayers of the Potosi Mint

Time Frame	Assayer Initial	Assayer Circa	Assayer Name	Features
Philip II reign 1556-1598 Potosi First Early Period	R	1574-1576	Alonso de Rincón	Commas in legend; double "P" in Philippus; Hispaniarum spelled Hisp or Isp; assayer and mint initials may appear to right of shield.
First Early Period	M	1576–1577	Possibly Miguel García	Commas in legend; double "P" in Philippus; Hispaniarum spelled Hisp or Isp; assayer and mint initials may appear to right of shield.
First Early Period	B	1577	Juan de Ballesteros Narváez	Commas in legend; double "P" in Philippus; Hispaniarum spelled Hisp or Isp.
Second Early Period	B Cont.	1578-1581	Juan de Ballesteros Narváez	Commas in legend; Double "P" in Philippus; Hisp or Isp; some w/ delicate pearls/diamonds border; broad "Great Module" coins appear.
Second Early Period	L	1578-1581	Probable lieutenant for Ballesteros	Commas in legend; double "P" in Philippus; Hisp or Isp.
Second Early Period	C	1579–1580	Probable lieutenant for Ballesteros	Commas in legend; double "P" in Philippus; Hispaniarum spelled Hisp or Isp.
Third Early Period	B	1581-1586	Juan de Ballesteros Narváez	Periods replace commas in legend; double "P" in Philippus; Hisp.
Third Early Period	A	1586-1589	Juan Álvarez Reinaltes	Periods in legend; double "P" in Philippus; Hisp.
Pre-Transition Period	B	1589-1598	Juan de Ballesteros Narváez/ Hernando Ballesteros	Introduction of horse-like lions, replaced by heavier "marching" lions; borders of dots, x's and/or squares; single or double "P" in Philipus.
Pre-Transition Period	R and RL/RBL monogram	1590–1598	Baltasar Ramos Leceta for Juan de Ballesteros Narváez	Small R, often pointed, and small RL/RBL monogram; introduction of horse-like lions, replaced by heavier "marching" lions; single or double "P" in Philipus.
King Philip II/III Transition	B and R continued	1598		Ordinal III begins on small R and small RL/RLB monogram coins. Extremely rare on this type.

14

Assayers of the Potosí Mint

Reign	Assayer mark	Dates	Assayer	Notes
Philip III reign 1598-1621 Post-Transition	B	1598–1605/10	Hernando Ballesteros for Juan de Ballesteros Narváez	Ordinal III begins on B assayer coins; x's and squares vanish; pearls/diamonds border common.
Post-Transition	B	1598-1610	Juan de Ballesteros Narváez	Ordinal III begins; x's and squares vanish; pearls/diamonds border common.
Post-Transition	R and RB/RL/RBL monogram	1598-1610	Baltasar Ramos Leceta for Ballesteros	Ordinal III begins; curved letter R and curved RB/RL/RBL monogram; pearls/diamonds border common.
	R	1610-1613	Baltasar Ramos Leceta alone	Ordinal III; curved R; pearls/diamonds border common; Sevilla-style castles begin to replace multi-windowed mansions; some with stars replacing fleurs-de-lis.
	C	Circa 1613	Name Unknown	Exceedingly rare
	Q	1613-1616	Agustín de la Quadra	Both multi-windowed and Sevilla style castles; both pearls/diamonds and dots borders; some with stars replacing fleurs-de-lis.
Dated Coins Begin	M	1616-1617	Juan Muñoz	1617, first dates on Potosi coins; die transpositions associated with assayer T begin to appear.
Assayer Transition	PARL monogram	1618	García de Paredes y Ulloa	Interim assayer; both large and small monograms.
Assayer Transition	monogram with T	1618	Dual Assayers: Tapia with Monogram Assayer	Monogram to left; T to right. Scarce.
Assayer Transition	T over monogram	1618	Juan Ximénez de Tapia	Extremely rare.
	T	1618-1621	Juan Ximénez de Tapia	Many die transpositions.
King Philip III/IV Transition	T continued	1621		
Philip IV reign 1621-1665	T	1621-Post 1622 sinking	Juan Ximénez de Tapia	Ordinal IIII; Many die transpositions.
	P	1622-Post 1622 sinking	Pedro Martín de Palencia	Also, intermittently as lieutenant prior to 1622.

Coins of the Mexico City Mint

Coins of the Mexico City mint are easily identifiable because each of the cross's four flared extensions ends in an orb – a symbol of royal authority. Typically cargo of the New Spain fleet, they are rarities on 1622 *Tierra Firme* fleet shipwrecks. The Mexico City mint began issuing coins during the monarchy of Johanna and Charles I (reign 1516-1556), almost four decades earlier than Potosi. Mexico coins produced from 1536 to circa 1572 display a pillars design with the motto *Plus Ultra*. Circa 1572 the crowned shield obverse replaced the pillars design. Mexico City mint coins beginning with the reign of Philip II include the ordinal number. The Mexico City mint added the year of issue to the coin legend—on the obverse—in 1607. The mint mark is a small o above M.

Mexico City mint, extremely rare Second Early Period, pillars with waves 2 reales coin, assayer initial L to right of shield

Mexico City mint, extremely rare 1 reale, partial date -607 over GRATIA

Mexico City mint, shield-style 8 reales coin, assayer A over F, with a full date of 1608

Assayers of the Mexico City Mint

Time Frame	Assayer Initial	Assayer Circa	Assayer Name	Features
Charles and Johanna reign 1515–1556 First Early Period	R	1536-1538	Francisco del Rincón	First minted coins of the Americas Pillars without waves; Legend: CAROLVS ET IOHANA REGES or REG or REGS or RE.
First Early Period	P	1538-1543	Pedro de Espina	Pillars without waves; CAROLVS ET IOHANA REGES with various spellings.
First Early Period	F	1539-1541	Francisco de Loaiza	Pillars without waves, CAROLVS ET IOHANA REGES with various spellings.
First Early Period	G	1539-1543	Juan Gutiérrez	Pillars without waves; CAROLVS ET IOHANA REGES with various spellings.
Second Early Period	S	1543-1544	Rodrigo Gómez de Santillán	Pillars with waves begin; CAROLVS ET IOHANA REGES with various spellings.
Second Early Period	A	1543-1544	Alonso de Villaseca?	Pillars with waves; CAROLVS ET IOHANA REGES with various spellings.
Second Early Period	R	1543-1544	Alonso Rincón	Pillars with waves; CAROLVS ET IOHANA REGES with various spellings.
Second Early Period	G	1544-1548	Juan Gutiérrez	Pillars with waves; CAROLVS ET IOHANA REGES with various spellings.
Second Early Period	L	1548-1556	Luis Rodríguez	Pillars with waves; CAROLVS ET IOHANA REGES with various spellings.
Charles and Johanna/Philip II Transition	L cont.	1556		
Philip II reign 1556-1598 Second Early Period	L	1556-1567	Luis Rodríguez	Pillars with waves; legend continues as CAROLVS ET IOHANA.
Second Early Period	O	1564-1572	Bernardo de Oñate	Pillars with waves; legend continues as CAROLVS ET IOHANA.

Assayers of the Mexico City Mint

Third Early Period	O	1572-1589	Bernardo de Oñate	Shield obverse begins; eight reales denominations begin; pearls/diamonds border common; Philippus with double "P" and ordinal II.
Third Early Period	O	1578-1589	Luis de Oñate	Pearls/diamonds border common; Philippus with double "P" and ordinal II.
Third Early Period	F	1589-1598	Francisco de Morales	Pearls/diamonds border common; Philippus with double "P" and ordinal II.
Philip II/III Transition	F with D	1598/1599	Francisco de Morales with Francisco de Quintana Dueñas	F with D coins with ordinal II and with ordinal III.
Philip III reign 1598-1621	F	1599-1606	Francisco de Morales	Pearls/diamonds border common; Philipus with single or double "P" and ordinal III.
Dated coins begin	F	1607-1608	Francisco de Morales	Dates appear on Mexico mint coins 1607; pearls/diamonds border common.
	A	1608–1610	Antonio de Morales, son of Francisco	Pearls/diamonds border common; Philipus with single or double "P" and ordinal III.
	F	1610–1618	Francisco de Morales	Both pearls/diamonds and dots borders; ordinal III; single or double "P" in Philipus.
	D	1618-1621	Diego de Godoy	Both pearls/diamonds and dots borders; ordinal III; single or double "P" in Philipus.
Philip IV reign 1621-1665	D	1621-Post 1622 sinking	Diego de Godoy	Ordinal IIII.

Treasure Coins ◊ Carol Tedesco

Coins of the Lima, Peru Mint

The Lima mint began producing coins in 1568 and operated sporadically, closing completely from 1572 to 1577, opening again from 1577 to 1588. There may have been one more brief effort at production in 1592 before closing for the remainder of the century, not to reopen until more than halfway through the next, long after the 1622 fleet losses.

Some years previous to the discovery of the *Atocha* and *Santa Margarita* shipwrecks, a prominent expert in the field of Spanish Colonial numismatics incorrectly attributed the coins of early Potosi assayers R, M, B, and L to the Lima mint, an error that was perpetuated by others citing his work. When you compare the workmanship, stylistic features, and artistic rendering of early Potosi with early Lima coins, it is easy to understand how their appearance contributed to this incorrect attribution. Eventually, archival documents came to light that corrected and reassigned the attributions. This is why Lima mint coins turned out to be considerably more rare on these shipwrecks than was originally believed, and also why what is actually an early Potosi mint coin might have been originally documented as one from Lima.

The rare Lima mint coins found on the *Atocha* and *Santa Margarita* —with the D assayer "Star of Lima" coins being amongst the most coveted in the entire collection—were struck during the reign of King Philip II and display a P mintmark, for Peru. The early pillars with waves type coins include the ordinal II in the legend; the shield types do not. None of the legends include a date.

Coins of the Lima Peru Mint

First Early Period Lima mint, assayer R, pillars with waves 4 reales coin

Second Early Period Lima mint, assayer X, 2 reales coin

"Star of Lima" 8 reales coin, assayer D to right of shield, star above Arabic 8 to left

Assayers of the Lima, Peru Mint

Time Frame	Assayer Initial	Assayer Circa	Assayer Name	Features
Philip II reign 1556-1598 First Early Period	R	1568-1570	Alonso de Rincón	Pillars with Waves
Second Early Period	X	1570-1572	Xinés Martínez	Pillars with Waves
Third Early Period	X	1572	Xinés Martínez	Shield obverse begins
Third Early Period	D	1577-1588	Diego de la Torre	Star of the Magi on most; multiple varieties; 2 reales predominate; mint/assayer initials appear to left or right of shield.

Exceedingly Rare Mint Specimens ~ New World

Panama City mint, assayer o above b, 2 reales coin

The Panama City mint operated for fewer than three years, between 1580 and 1583.

Pictured here is one of only two known examples from the *Atocha*, both of which are assayer o above b (name unknown) to left of shield, AP mintmark above denomination II to right.

Santa Fe de Bogotá, 2 reales coin, full date 1622, incongruent ordinal III

Santa Fe de Bogotá, assayer A to right of shield, 4 reales coin

Cartagena, 8 reales coin

Both the Santa Fe de Bogotá and the Cartagena, Columbia mints began production in 1622, under the establishment of military engineer Don Alonso Turrillo de Yebra. Originally each of the types shown were attributed to Santa Fe de Bogotá, until archival research confirmed the existence of an ancillary mint in Cartagena. Of the scant hand-full recovered, those 1622 issues with R above N to the left of the shield and having no pomegranate to represent New Granada have been attributed to Cartagena, and those 1622 issues with S above F or S alone to the left of the shield and having a pomegranate to represent New Granada are attributed to Santa Fe de Bogotá. With the exception of the 2 reales denominations, the assayer initial A appears on coins of both mints. All include the Portuguese arms within the shield—upper third, center.

Exceedingly Rare Mint Specimens ~ Old World

The purpose of the 1622 *Tierra Firme* fleet was to transport the riches of the Americas (the New World) to Europe (the Old World). Old World coins discovered on *Tierra Firme* fleet, 1622 shipwrecks were twice-traveled wealth, having originated in Europe, traveled over the ocean to the New World, and were now en route back to Europe. In 1580, Philip II expanded his empire with the addition of the Portuguese throne, after which the Portuguese arms were incorporated into the shield.

Seville, 8 reales coin, (circa 1588-1591; pre-Portuguese arms) assayer P just below the three o'clock position on the coin reverse

Seville, 4 reales coin, assayer reversed D (intermittently circa 1612-1621), ordinal IIII

While exceedingly scarce relative to the collection as a whole, among Old World coins on the 1622 *Tierra Firme* fleet shipwrecks, those from Seville have the greatest representation — which is not surprising as the port of Seville was the hub for all commerce to and from the "Indies." Dots and/or dashes may embellish the flag of Austria or surround the fleur-de-lys of Burgundy. The second mint of the city of Seville, which operated from before 1497 until 1586, still stands today.

Granada, 2 reales coin, assayer M (circa 1597-1621)

The Granada mint issued its first coins in the year 1492. Discovered on the *Atocha*, the one pictured is one of only two confirmed specimens from the *Atocha/Margarita* collection, and the only one with a visible assayer initial.

Madrid, 4 reales coin, assayer V, (circa 1621)
partial date xx21, ordinal III

The Madrid mint began issuing coins in 1615. Discovered on the Atocha, the one pictured is the one confirmed specimen from the *Atocha/Margarita* collection.

Exceedingly Rare Mint Specimens

Segovia, 8 reales coin, assayer IM, reign of Phillip II

The aqueduct symbol is the mintmark for Segovia mint coins. In 1585, a new mint with machinery to produce the first machine-made Spanish coins opened in Segovia. The coin pictured here, discovered on the Atocha, was struck at the "Old Segovia" mint, which continued to produce hand-struck coins exclusively, and is the only confirmed silver specimen from the Atocha/Margarita collection.

Toledo, 8 reales coin, assayer P, full date 1621

The Toledo mint began issuing coins during the reign of Isabella and Ferdinand II (1474-1504) and moved to its final location in 1504. This building still stands today. The coin pictured here is one of seven confirmed silver Toledo mint coins from the *Atocha/Margarita* collection. Five are assayer P (intermittently circa 1615-1621); one (*Santa Margarita*) is an assayer C (intermittently circa 1591-1616); and one is circled M assayer (circa 1590).

Exceedingly Rare Mint Specimens ~ Gold Coins

Gold coins, called escudos by the Spanish and popularly nicknamed "doubloons," have been discovered on both the *Atocha* and the *Santa Margarita* shipwrecks, but in scant numbers; fewer than 150 on the Atocha; less than 60 on the *Santa Margarita*. Several of the very first gold coins minted in the Americas were on the 1622 fleet shipwrecks—but the story of gold is another story…

Se Acaba

Acknowledgements

This book has been excerpted from my expanded study: *Pieces of Eight ~ Silver Treasure Coins of the 1622 Shipwrecks Nuestra Senora de Atocha, Santa Margarita & the Portuguese Carrack São José*. Without the contributions of those credited below, neither would have come to fruition.

My thanks go out to Mel, Deo, and the Fisher family for sharing the dream. I am grateful to Mel Fishers Treasures, Inc., (MFT) President and CEO Kim Fisher, MFT Vice President and Director of Marketing Sean Fisher, and Mel Fisher Center, Inc., President Taffi Fisher-Abt for their generosity in sharing their documentation, and to Taffi in particular for her assistance and passionate interest in my ongoing research—and for urging me to publish an abridged edition specific to the coins of the *Atocha* and the *Santa Margarita*. Many thanks to MFT Curator Sandy Kavanaugh and Media Liaison Sharon Wiley for their help in assembling coin images, to Gary Randolph, V.P. of Operations for his ongoing support, and to Senior Conservator John Corcoran for his valuable insights.

Photographs of coins from the important *Atocha* research collection are a key contribution to *Pieces of Eight ~ Silver Treasure Coins of the 1622 Shipwrecks Nuestra Senora de Atocha, Santa Margarita & the Portuguese Carrack São José*, and access to the research of the late Henry Taylor was an important component to my earliest education in Spanish Colonial coin lore. For these contributions I thank the Mel Fisher Maritime Heritage Society, in particular Chief Archaeologist Corey Malcom, who introduced me to Mr. Taylor's numismatic notes and to Dylan Kibler, Registrar/Photographer, for his great patience in assembling and proving photographs of the research collection coins. Monica Brook, Conservator, is also to be thanked for her many contributions.

Thanks are due to past Executive Director Dr. Madeleine Burnside, whose support made the contributions of these individual's possible; and to present Executive Director Melissa Kendrick for continuing that tradition.

Thank you to Daniel Huntington, Numismatic Guaranty Corporation, for your insight regarding assayer initial placement on some Philip II reign, Seville mint coins.

Suggested Reading

A True Relation of that Which Lately Hapned to the great Spanish Fleet, and Galleons of Terra Firma in America, London, 1623, edited by Ernie Richards

Cobs, Pieces of Eight and Treasure Coins, Sewall Menzel

The Coinage of El Peru, essays edited by William L. Bischoff: *Documentary Evidence Regarding the La Plata Mint and the First Issues of Potosi*, Arnaldo J. Cunietti-Ferrando

The First Assayers at Potosi, K. A. Dym

The Forgotten Mint of Colonial Panama, Jorge A. Proctor

The Practical Book of Cobs, Daniel Sedwick and Frank Sedwick

Numismatica Española, F. Calicó, X. Calicó and J. Trigo

8 Reales Cobs of Potosi, Emilio Paoletti

Las acuñaciones de las cecas de Lima, La Plata y Potosi 1568 – 1651, Dr. E. A. Sellschopp

Steel and Die Making for New World Hand-Hammered Coins, article published in the Journal of the Professional Treasure Hunter, November-December 1997, Douglas R. Armstrong

Treasure of the Atocha, Dr. R. Duncan Mathewson III

Search for the Motherlode of the Atocha, Dr. Eugene Lyon

The Spanish Treasure Fleets, Timothy B. Walton

The Log of Christopher Columbus, translated by Robert H. Fuson

Tales of Potosi, Bartolome Arzans de Orsua y Vela, edited by R.C. Padden, translated by Frances M. Lopez-Morillas

The Buccaneers of America, John Esquemeling

Treasure Coins ◊ *Carol Tedesco*

Recommended Web Sites

A Precolumbian Portfolio – Archive of photographs created by Justin Kerr: *research.mayavase.com/kerrportfolio.html*

Arqueonautas Worldwide: *arq.de*

Blazon Search: *blazonsearch.com*

Blue Water Ventures of Key West: *bwvkw.com*

EN RADA Publications: *enrada.com*

Foundation for the Advancement of Mesoamerican Studies, Inc.: *famsi.org*

Friends of the Segovia Mint: *segoviamint.org/Eng-start.htm*

Historic Research and Certification, Inc.: *lostgalleons.com*

Mel Fishers Treasures: *melfisherstreasures.com*

Odyssey Marine Exploration: *shipwreck.net*

The Library of Congress Rare Book & Special Collections Reading Room – The Jay I. Kislak Collection: *loc.gov/rr/rarebook/kislak.html*

The Mel Fisher Museum: *melfisher.org*

The Professional Marine Explorers Society: *professionalmarineexplorers.com*

X-Ray International Dive Magazine: *xray-mag.com*

Image Credits

Cover image: created c. 1630 by Henricus Hondius, Dutch mapmaker, (1597-1651).

The Conquest of Tenochtitlán, artist unknown: Library of Congress Prints and Photographs Division Washington, Jay I. Kislak Collection, D.C./Public domain

Motherload image: courtesy of Don Kincaid, © Don Kincaid. All rights reserved.

Research Collection coins photographed by Scott Neirling, © Mel Fisher Maritime Heritage Society. All rights reserved.

Mel Fishers Treasures, Inc., coin photographs courtesy of Mel Fishers Treasures, Inc., © Mel Fishers Treasures, Inc. All rights reserved.

About the Author

Carol Tedesco is an internationally recognized Spanish Colonial coin expert and historic shipwreck professional who has worked with projects in North America, South America, the Caribbean, Africa, and the Pacific. She has curated tens of thousands of coins and is considered the foremost authority on 1622 fleet treasure coins. With a diverse résumé that includes historic shipwreck research, search and recovery, documentary and fine art photography, and media and public relations, her accomplishments have been recognized by the Who's Who of Entrepreneurs and with membership in the Explorers Club. A published author of several investigative archaeological mystery articles, Carol is a popular speaker throughout the country on the subject of sunken galleons and their treasures. Today, Carol consults for some of the most prominent historic shipwreck search and recovery companies in the world. She lives in Key West, Florida, with her partner Michael Shields and two black and white tuxedo cats named Buster and Bleu.

Carol is a Founding Member of the Professional Marine Explorers Society and encourages those who support both responsible, professional private sector shipwreck search and recovery and cooperative efforts among private and public sector organizations to join as well. For more information on ProMES, visit: www.professionalmarineexplorers.com.

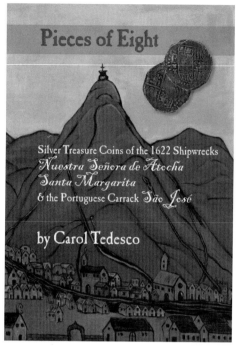

The contents of this booklet are excerpted from *Pieces of Eight ~ Silver Treasure Coins of the 1622 Shipwrecks Nuestra Senora de Atocha, Santa Margarita & the Portuguese Carrack São José,*" Carol Tedesco 2011, published by SeaStory Press, Key West, Florida, USA, and may not be reproduced in print or electronically, in whole or in part, without express permission of the publisher and author.

With cover art-work by Kate Peachey

Visit lostgalleons.com for information on availability

Publishers Note: *Fully illustrated with hundreds of finely detailed photographs, Pieces of Eight is more than just a reference book. Carol Tedesco not only explains the subtle nuances of the coins themselves in fascinating detail, but places them in the context of their moment in history, explaining where they were coming from, where they were going, and why.*

Authors Note: The data for the assayer years and features included in *Treasure Coins of the Nuestra Senora de Atocha and the Santa Margarita* has been derived from study of the most current and authoritive resources and from my own experience and observations. Note that the Portuguese carrack *São José* which sank off of Africa in 1622—though carrying coins from the same mints—produced varieties unknown on the *Atocha* and *Santa Margarita* shipwrecks. *Pieces of Eight ~ Silver Treasure Coins of the 1622 Shipwrecks Nuestra Senora de Atocha, Santa Margarita & the Portuguese Carrack São José* includes these varieties.